Original title:
Peachy Pathways

Copyright © 2025 Creative Arts Management OÜ
All rights reserved.

Author: Aurora Sinclair
ISBN HARDBACK: 978-1-80586-466-0
ISBN PAPERBACK: 978-1-80586-938-2

## Sweet Trails of Reflection

A stroll through gardens lush and wide,
Where squirrels wear top hats with pride.
Bumblebees buzz in a conga line,
While daisies dance, feeling just divine.

I tripped on a root and did a pirouette,
Landed in a patch of spaghetti wet.
Tomatoes laughed, and carrots rolled,
Even the onions looked mildly consoled.

The sunbeams pranced on a mini parade,
As rhubarb insisted it should serenade.
Cabbages jived, with kohlrabi in tow,
They formed a conga of veggie tableau.

As twilight fell with a giggle and cheer,
I waved goodbye to the frolicking sphere.
Napping on cushions of perfectly ripe,
Fruit-filled dreams, I'm prepared for a type!

## Roads Fringed with Foliage and Fruit

Bananas wearing hats are quite the sight,
Apples doing the tango, oh what a night.
Berries in limbo, swaying away,
Fruits having fun, come join the play.

Citrus on scooters racing like mad,
Grapes in a parade, the funniest fad.
Melons jump-rope, and they never fall,
Nature's comedy show, it's a ball!

## Essence of the Softest Breezes

Mangoes whisper secrets in gentle tones,
Kiwi sings ballads, far from their homes.
Pineapples giggle, spinning around,
Tickled by breezes, laughter is found.

Watermelon dreams sweetly afloat,
Cherry blossoms dance, wearing a coat.
Peaches perform on a warm summer day,
With laughter and joy, they wiggle away.

## Journeying Among Juicy Delights

Raspberries roller-skate with flair,
Cherries on swings soar high in the air.
Plums ride bicycles, oh what a show,
Juicy delights, always on the go!

Lemonade lakes where ducks paddle through,
Cantaloupe castles under skies so blue.
Tangerines play hopscotch on the ground,
In this quirky land, fun's all around!

## Sun-kissed Moments on Winding Paths

Peppers prance in sun's golden glow,
Cucumbers conquer the dance floor below.
Zucchini wears sunglasses, striking a pose,
As carrots cheer on with their orange clothes.

Cherry pies giggle, sharing their dreams,
While smoothies swirl, bursting with beams.
Toasting to sunshine, they make quite a scene,
On these wacky paths, life feels like a dream!

## **Treading on Nature's Candy**

Walking on a fruit parade,
Every step, a squished cascade.
Careful now, don't lose your shoes,
Nature's treats come with some blues.

Sipping juice from the air,
Sunshine shines, but watch your hair!
Bouncing bugs, they join the fun,
I tripped on bliss, oh what a run.

### Light and Lush Beneath the Sky


Stumbling through a squishy dream,
Underneath a golden beam.
Pull a leaf, it's quite a splash,
Oops! I made a sticky dash.

Bouncing on this vibrant floor,
Wiggly critters asking for more.
Nature laughs and so do I,
As jelly beans fall from the sky.

## Footprints Amidst Glistening Corridors

Slipping on the joy so sweet,
Every corner, a tasty treat.
Racing through this wobbly maze,
Giggling at the fruit's wild ways.

Grinning as I trip once more,
These shiny paths I can't ignore.
Kicking pebbles, what a scene,
Life's a peachy, juicy dream.

**Citrus Serenity Under the Stars**

Dancing under a juicy glow,
Stars above, but who's to know?
Slicing through the night with ease,
Swinging from my citrus trees.

Dreamy scents fill the cool air,
Fluttering bugs—do they care?
Laughter spills like sweetened wine,
In this night of fruit divine.

## Soft Pink Trails of Curiosity

Gentle whispers in the air,
Curiosity leads us there.
With every step, a giggle bursts,
Exploring paths that quench our thirst.

Bouncing off the soft-cut grass,
Who knew that squirrels could be so sass?
Chasing shadows, making friends,
On this trail, laughter never ends.

## Seasonal Smiles on Winding Roads

Colors change with silly grace,
Each turn reveals a new fun face.
Laughter dances on the tress,
As nature plays a game of chess.

Autumn leaves in hats of gold,
Tell secrets that never get old.
With every rustle, a new delight,
On this road, the fun feels right.

## Tasting the Early Evening Breeze

Evening whispers, warm and sweet,
Breezy laughter, a tasty treat.
Crisp apples call from trees so tall,
Float along, let worries fall.

The sun winks, a cheeky star,
Boys race bikes, oh, how they spar!
With every breeze, they claim the night,
Making memories, pure delight.

## Beneath the Canopy of Dreams

Underneath the branches wide,
Wonders bloom where dreams reside.
Squirrels play peek-a-boo with light,
In this realm, the world feels right.

With shadows dancing on the ground,
A giggle-filled treasure can be found.
Sharing secrets with the breeze,
Life is silly, if you please.

**Fragrant Forays through Blossoms**

In gardens where bees buzz and tease,
The flowers wear dresses, swaying with ease.
A rabbit in shades, sunglasses on tight,
Sips nectar smoothies, oh, what a sight!

Dancing squirrels in a flower-filled chase,
Juggling blueberries, a messy embrace.
Their laughter's contagious under the sun,
In this floral affair, we frolic and run.

## **Pathways of Incandescent Joy**

A road lined with giggles, a skip in my feet,
With candy-striped sidewalks and berry-sweet treats.
The sun wears a grin, and clouds are all fluffy,
While ducks with top hats look ever so stuffy.

We slide down the rainbows, we bounce off the grass,
With balloons in our hands, oh, how the hours pass!
Chasing the sunshine, we dance with delight,
In this realm of wonder, everything feels right.

## Sweetness Under a Canopy

Under the trees where the candy rains fall,
We lounge on gumdrops, the best seats of all.
A piñata parade, it's a sight to behold,
With confetti and laughter, as sweet times unfold.

In this sugary haven, with snacks piled high,
A chocolate chip mountain reaching up to the sky.
We munch on our dreams, all cozy and bright,
With giggles and crunches through day and through night.

## Where the Warmth Beckons

Where the sun pulls a chair and whispers a tune,
A dance of the daisies beneath the warm moon.
We toast marshmallow ghosts and share silly tales,
While our friendship sets sail, catching whimsical gales.

In hidden nooks where the bright colors play,
Frogs wear bow ties, and sing through the day.
The warmth wraps around like a well-worn quilt,
In this joyous escape, all worries are spilt.

## Sunlit Trails of Delight

Bouncing on the sandy way,
Chasing light, we laugh and play.
Candy trees that grow so high,
We'll taste the clouds as we fly.

Bicycles with squeaky wheels,
Riding through those purple peels.
Banana splits and silly hats,
Tickling strangers; look at that!

Jumping over little streams,
Waking up from sunny dreams.
Giggles echo down the lane,
Chasing shadows, feel no pain.

Friends all gathered under skies,
Lemonade and firefly spies.
A treasure map marked by doodles,
Summer's gold that brightly noodles.

## **Golden Fruit and Gentle Roads**

On the road where sunshine beams,
Fruity laughter fuels our dreams.
Pineapple hats and mango swings,
Life's a carnival of things.

Riding waves, oh what a sight,
Jellyfish jump in pure delight.
Squeaky shoes and watermelon,
This path is ours, no need for zen.

Skating past the jelly jars,
We're the kings of candy bars.
Lemon drops rain from above,
On this road, we push and shove.

Rides on scooters, wheels that glide,
Come along for the silly ride.
Laughter dances in the breeze,
Life is sweet like honey bees.

## Sweet Surrender of Summer

In a field of candy blooms,
Bubbles float in giant rooms.
Hand in hand, we trip and slip,
On a juicy, fruity trip.

Bouncing on a giant peach,
Tickled by the summer's reach.
Ice-cream trucks and silly songs,
Join us now as we sing along.

Chasing butterflies in flight,
Hopping under the sunlight.
Open hearts and carefree minds,
Summer's treasure softly finds.

With each game that we ignite,
Laughter dances day and night.
A picnic where the ants parade,
Making memories in this glade.

## The Warmth of Fragrant Breezes

Lazy days in a cotton haze,
Fragrant flowers start to blaze.
Snack attacks in the sunset glow,
Chasing echoes, to and fro.

Gather 'round, it's time to feast,
Donut holes for every beast.
Lemonade with funny straws,
Life is sweet, no need for laws.

Silly dances in the grass,
Clouds above begin to pass.
Giggling as we eat our fill,
Summer vibes, let's take a thrill.

Bonfire bright and marshmallow skies,
With our friends, the joy just flies.
Tickling tales that never end,
On this path, we all transcend.

## Harvested Hues and Wanderlust

In fields where colors brightly clash,
Peaches tumble in a goofy crash.
Farmers dance with baskets wide,
Their hats fly off, take on a ride!

A squirrel steals a juicy treat,
With nimble paws, it can't be beat.
The sun smiles down, a playful glee,
While birds join in a comical spree!

The tractor sputters, then it chokes,
As laughter echoes, bursting folks.
With sticky hands and full, round cheeks,
We savor summer's silly peaks.

So here's to harvest, wild and fun,
Where laughter lingers like the sun.
In fields of joy, we wander free,
With every bite, a giggle spree!

## Aromas of the Gentle Slope

A breeze of sweetness takes a turn,
As bees perform their dance, they churn.
The air is thick with fruity cheer,
While deck chairs wobble — oh dear, oh dear!

With picnic spreads that boast and tease,
A sandwich slips — oh what a breeze!
Peach juice splashes, it's quite a sight,
As giggles fill the warm, bright night.

A hedgehog snorts, an awkward scene,
Chasing a pickle — what does it mean?
Laughter bubbles from every nook,
As friends gather 'round to tell the book.

On gentle slopes, the fun won't stop,
We roll, we tumble, and then we plop.
With every mouthful, joy takes flight,
In this fragrant, funny, silly light!

## A Tapestry of Flavor and Light

A patchwork quilt of taste and hue,
Where fruit is ripe and laughter's too.
Each bite a burst, each giggle shared,
Fruit fly swats are comically bared.

We twirl through scents that tickle the nose,
With pastry chefs and funny prose.
The oven puffs like balloons of fun,
As aprons droop — oh, isn't this a run?

Mixing bowls spill with reckless flair,
A dash of love, with some playful air.
The kitchen's chaos, a sight so rare,
With flour clouds up high — we're unaware!

In this vibrant spice of laughter's art,
We bake together, each taking part.
Through flavors bright, and moments light,
Our culinary dreams take flight!

## Serene Strolls Through Lush Delights

Beneath the arch of leafy trees,
We wander forth with a buzz and breeze.
A squirrel chats while doing squats,
As nature giggles, oh, what a plot!

The paths are lined with blooms so bright,
Each step we take feels just so right.
A pot of jam rolls down the lane,
As slippery jokes bounce off the grain.

With picnic baskets tucked in tow,
We sip on drinks with a vibrant glow.
A little fern does a jig in the grass,
As frogs croak laughter, let time pass!

So stroll with me through fields of joy,
Where nature's humor we can enjoy.
With every step, a funny tale,
In lush delights, our spirits sail!

## Radiant Blossoms and Quiet Roads

On a crooked lane where daisies shout,
A llama in shades dances about.
Bumblebees buzz with a loud, silly tune,
While squirrels play chess with a raccoon.

Jellybeans drop from the sky like rain,
Neighbors argue over sugar cane.
Giddy laughter fills the air so bright,
As the sun gives a wink with pure delight.

## **Where Summer Blooms**

Under a beach ball that floats like a kite,
A goat in flip-flops takes flight in delight.
Watermelons roll into the picnic scene,
As ants wear sunglasses, looking quite keen.

Old Mr. Frog plays the clarinet,
While seagulls compete in a silly duet.
Sandcastles crumble, a majestic retreat,
As the tide giggles and dances on feet.

## A Symphony of Ripening Fruits

Bananas harmonize in a fruity rap,
While oranges form a cheeky, tight slap.
A bowler hat floats atop a ripe pear,
As grapes do somersaults, full of flair.

Mangoes wear bow ties to strut their stuff,
Peaches giggle, saying, 'We've had enough!'
A pineapple juggles, quite full of zest,
All while a cucumber, crashing the fest.

## Melody of the Orchard Breeze

In an orchard where trees start to sing,
A chicken on roller skates does its thing.
Crisp apples gossip with radishes bold,
As a strawberry tells tales of pure gold.

The wind makes a flute from branches so high,
Bananas wear wigs, making clouds pass by.
Funky fruit parties under the sun,
As nature joins in, and oh what fun!

## Sunlit Relics of a Gentle Path

Under the sun, we prance and play,
Where daisies giggle and children sway.
Old shoes lost on the grassy stretch,
Leave memories that we always fetch.

Path lined with laughter, a soft parade,
Where squirrels scamper, and sunlight's laid.
A dog with a stick, so proud and loud,
He thinks he's the king, we're all his crowd.

A breeze whisks by, tickles our nose,
As we chase shadows where the daisies grow.
Each twist and turn brings a silly cheer,
With every step, more laughter near.

Only on this road, where joy won't stop,
Do we find the candy in the lollipop.
So let's skip along with a giggling song,
On sunlit relics, where we belong.

**Constellations among the Blossoms**

Under a sky of cotton-candy dreams,
We dance by flowers, hear their beams.
Stars in petals, twinkling bright,
Telling tales of a whimsical night.

Bees in bow ties, buzzing with flair,
Doing their jig without a care.
Dandelions wish upon chubby bees,
While ants march by, dressed to appease.

Oh, what a sight, all colors collide,
In our merry garden, where giggles abide.
A romping rabbit hops in a top hat,
Inviting all to join in his chat.

So we lie back, in this floral sea,
Counting stars as they dance with glee.
Laughter and petals, both softly twine,
Constellations among the blossoms, divine.

**Fruity Fantasies on Winding Paths**

On winding paths paved with fruity fun,
Where watermelon waves greet the sun.
Beneath the trees, where we giggle and glide,
Jellybean bunnies bounce in their pride.

A lemon's a taxi, taking us far,
As grapes roll by, driving a car.
We toss around cherries, just like a game,
While a pineapple shouts, "Hey, who's to blame?"

Fruits of our labor, we sing and spin,
A party where chaos is where we begin.
Blueberries dancing in jiggly delight,
In this fruity realm, everything feels right.

Each twist in the path, a new flavor to taste,
With giggles and laughter, there's never a waste.
So come join the jest on this magical road,
Fruity fantasies lighten our load.

## Rustic Roads of Aroma and Color

Down rustic roads where the wild herbs sway,
We stroll in a fragrance, bright as the day.
Basil and thyme whisper secrets so neat,
Inviting us on, to their aromatic feat.

A parade of colors, a rainbow of greens,
Where grasshopper symphonies play in between.
Tomatoes wear hats, all plump and round,
While onions make jokes, in layers they're found.

Every corner we turn, a burst of delight,
With carrots who march in a row, just right.
The scent of fresh bread floating in air,
Tempts us to linger, oh, wouldn't we dare?

So let's wander on these paths, full of cheer,
With flavors and laughter that draw us near.
On rustic roads, where the sun brightly beams,
We find the essence of our silliest dreams.

## Drifting in a Garden of Abundance

In rows of fuzzy treasures, they shine,
A fruit parade, oh so divine.
With every bite, a giggle's found,
As juice drips down, laughter's abound.

Squirrels plotting, their snack heist grand,
Forget the nuts, it's fruity land!
With silly hats, and bright balloons,
We dance beneath the ripening moons.

Gardening mishaps, a comedy streak,
Those tomatoes shout, 'We're not for the weak!'
Mischief blooms in the sunny glade,
Nature's jesters, in green masquerade.

So grab a basket, join the fun,
Under the rays, we all become one.
In this garden, the giggles soar,
With every fruit, there's room for more!

## Lush Hues of a Sunlit Voyage

On a journey of colors, we merrily roam,
Waving at trees, calling each 'home.'
Strawberries wink with a cheeky glow,
'Pick us now, or miss the show!'

Banana boats floating in the breeze,
Bouncing like kids, swaying with ease.
Orange suns laughing atop the hill,
While grape clusters spill with delightful thrill.

Watermelons blush with bashful delight,
'Come taste our sweetness, it's quite a sight!'
Bees buzzing jokes, pollens collide,
Laughter is nectar that's hard to hide.

So let's sail forth, with a fruit-filled map,
Where mischief awaits in every hap.
Under the magic of a sunlit sky,
Adventures await, just give it a try!

## The Allure of Hidden Trails

Through winding paths, the secrets dwell,
Fruit whispers stories, oh what a swell.
Berries blush red, ripe for a tease,
With giggles echoing through swaying trees.

Mischievous critters, donning their best,
Throwing a party, they never rest.
The apples throw shade, they've got quite the view,
While neighbors argue, who's the juiciest crew.

As we stroll deeper, the laughter grows,
Strawberries gossip in swirls and flows.
'Find the hidden treasure!' they slyly claim,
While oranges roll in a fruity game.

So wander along, let your spirit fly,
Through these merry trails, friendship will spry.
In the gleeful chaos, we find our way,
To laughter, to joy, in the fruited ballet!

## Whispering Winds and Fruity Dreams

The winds giggle softly as they sway,
Tickling flowers in a playful ballet.
'Come join the feast!' the breeze does tease,
Where apples and pears dance with ease.

In a land of whimsy, where fruits have flair,
Bananas in pajamas, floating mid-air.
Cherries throw parties in the shade,
With berry confetti, by nature made.

Kites made of oranges whisk through the beam,
Tangled in laughter, in this fruity dream.
Each gust brings tickles and sweet surprises,
A festival of flavors, oh how it rises!

So take a deep breath, let joy entwine,
In this garden of giggles, where all is fine.
With each fruity whisper, embrace the cheer,
And dance through the day, with dreams crystal clear!

## Collecting Moments of Soft Warmth

In a land of fuzzy fruit, so sweet,
I tripped on a gnome with tiny feet.
Chasing laughter wrapped in sun,
I slipped on slime—oh, what fun!

Giggles float like fluff in air,
A squirrel stole my picnic, I swear!
With juice dribbling down my chin,
I guess it's time to dive right in!

Banana peels and wobbly chairs,
Here comes a cart of jelly bears!
Rolling downhill in a fruit parade,
Look out, world! It's a slippery spade!

Crimson cheeks from laughing too hard,
I may have cried—just not a shard.
With memories ripe, and cheeks all rosy,
Who's got my lunch? Oh, it's so cozy!

## Trails Lined with Breezy Hues

On a trail of jelly beans I stroll,
Finding candy wrappers, what a toll!
Breezy winds tease my hair in tangles,
Every twist and turn, my laughter wrangles.

Colors of giggles in yellow and green,
Dancing with daisies, a whimsical scene.
I met a fungi, it winked—how bold!
Said, "Stay a while, let your stories unfold!"

I'm skipping along on marshmallow dreams,
With gummy bears plotting their schemes.
Who knew delight could grow on trees?
Well, not these ones, just some bees!

I stumbled upon a pineapple hat,
That promised me riches—a tasty chat!
Riding the breeze, with giggles in tow,
No map needed, just go with the flow!

## A Journey through Liquid Sunshine

Lemonade rivers flow down the lane,
With rubber ducks dancing, insane!
I slipped on sugar, fell with a splash,
Giggling fish swam with quite the dash!

A sunbeam tickled my toes and knees,
While lollipops whispered sweet melodies.
With a laugh and a cheer, I catapulted high,
Jumped into cupcakes—oh my, oh my!

Jellyfish floated in the guava air,
Each squishy bump made me laugh and stare.
In a puddle of sunshine, I paddled with flair,
Chasing sparkles that tingled my hair!

Onwards I skated to a candy land,
Where fun never faltered, always grand.
With each silly step in this fruity scene,
Life's just a cartoon, vivid and keen!

## Orchard Adventures Await

In an orchard of giggles, I frolic about,
With apples that wink and pears that shout.
I stumbled and tumbled, lost on my quest,
Only to find a fruit-throwing jest!

The trees are all dancing, can you believe?
I swear they're playing tricks up their sleeve!
Caught in a game of hide and seek,
A raspberry whispered, "Come join the freak!"

Cherries flying like confetti in spring,
Each burst of laughter—a sweet little thing.
Found a peach wearing sunglasses so cool,
Said, "Float on this breeze, forget the rule!"

I skipped with delight, in a world full of cheer,
Every twist of fruit brought giggles near.
Orchard magic, where mischief does play,
Adventure awaits—let's seize the day!

## Nectar Roads to Dreamland

Beneath the trees where giggles grow,
I trip on roots, my face aglow.
The bees will buzz, they dance with glee,
While I chase dreams like a bumblebee.

With sticky fingers, fruit in hand,
I roam through orchards, oh so grand.
A slippery slope, I take a slide,
And land on grass with graceful pride.

Here come the fairies, dressed in green,
Telling jokes that can't be seen.
They tickle me and make me laugh,
As I roll down a lemon path.

The clouds above begin to tease,
They look like jellybeans, if you please!
I shout aloud, "What a fine day!"
On nectar roads, I love to play.

## Orchard Whispers

In shades of pink, the blossoms sway,
They whisper secrets, come what may.
A squirrel chuckles, flips his tail,
As I dance around on berry trails.

The shadows giggle under trees,
With every rustle in the breeze.
I slip on strawberries, who knew?
This fruity path could be so blue!

Jellybeans rain from skies so wide,
I stick my tongue out, ready to ride.
Laughing birds draw doodles in flight,
Filling my heart with pure delight.

As night arrives, the stars will cheer,
With marshmallow dreams, far and near.
Under the moon, my worries flee,
In orchards where I'm wild and free.

## Melted Sunsets on Dusty Trails

The sun drips down like ice cream cones,
My feet feel light like silly stones.
Each sunset mess is quite a treat,
As I'm skipping on my wobbly feet.

Dusty trails lead to giggly falls,
Where laughter echoes, and time sprawls.
Chasing shadows of silly cats,
Who play hide and seek with all the bats.

Lemonade rivers, oh what a sight,
I dive right in, feeling just right.
With dandelions as my crown,
I paint the sunset, never down.

The day wraps up in a jelly hug,
While fireflies dance, I start to bug.
No serious thoughts at all, just glee,
On these trails where I'm meant to be.

## Petals Beneath My Feet

Waltzing on petals that twist and twirl,
With every step, my dreams unfurl.
A butterfly giggles, stuck in my hair,
As I prance about without a care.

The flowers whisper cheeky rhymes,
Counting my giggles, losing track of times.
Tulips tease as I aim to hop,
And land with a thud, like a funny plop!

Bouncing over tulips, oh what fun!
Chasing shadows of the setting sun.
The daisies chuckle, "What a delight!"
As I skip through fields, feeling so light.

With each soft petal beneath my shoes,
I dance and sing, in grape-flavored hues.
In a world so bright, nothing seems wrong,
In flower-filled meadows, I hum along.

## Fruity Footnotes in Nature's Diary

In the orchard where laughter grows,
Apples wink, and the cherry tree knows.
Bananas slip, with a giggle nearby,
And pears tell tales as the breeze starts to sigh.

Fruits play tricks on a sunny day,
Oranges giggle, they won't roll away.
Berries burst into fits of glee,
As we skip through this fruity spree.

Underneath leaves, the secrets unfold,
Grapes gossip sweetly, as stories are told.
Pineapples wear crowns, feeling quite grand,
In this fruity funland, all perfectly planned.

So laugh with the plants, let your worries decay,
Nature's diary's written in humorous play.
In the lanes of delight, let your heart take the lead,
For life is a garden, and laughter's the seed.

## Path of the Blushing Sun

On the trail where the sun likes to blush,
The daisies giggle, but the bees make a rush.
With shadows that dance, twirling around,
And leaves that rustle, soft joy abound.

The sun wears a smile, it's quite a sight,
Kissing the blooms with a golden light.
While butterflies flutter in the warm air,
Making dreams out of flowers beyond compare.

Squirrels tell jokes from high in the trees,
While ladybugs laugh in gentle breeze.
Crazy adventures await every turn,
With each little giggle, new joys we discern.

So walk on this road where the sun winks just right,
Join in the fun, share laughter and light.
For on this bright trail, oh what a spree,
Nature's a party, come dance with me!

## Forests of Fuzz and Flavor

In the woods where the fuzziness reigns,
Berries bounce, and the laughter remains.
Mushrooms giggle under the shade,
While the fruits of the forest join in the parade.

Kiwis dangle, playing peek-a-boo,
While raspberries toot their little horns too.
The leaves whisper secrets, so wild and unique,
In this fuzzy forest, it's joy that we seek.

The bushes chuckle, tickling our feet,
As pies in the sky sing a tune oh so sweet.
Nature's a dessert, with flavors galore,
In a land full of fun, who could ask for more?

So leap through the woods, let your worries go,
In forests of flavor, let laughter flow.
With fuzz all around and sweetness on high,
Join the fun dance, beneath the wide sky!

## Dancing Shadows Under Ripe Canopies

Underneath branches where shadows play,
Fruits are winking in a cheeky way.
Plums start a jig, while cherries sing loud,
In this sunny realm, they gather a crowd.

Bananas in hats, oh, what a sight!
While mangoes hum softly in warm golden light.
Coconuts chuckle as they swish and sway,
While shadows do salsa, just having their way.

Lemons drop puns, each zesty and bright,
As oranges tumble, oh, what a delight!
This canopy's party has no room for frowns,
With nature's own joy, we dance all around.

So join in the laughter, let your spirits soar,
Under ripe canopies, there's always much more.
In this whimsical world where the funny things bloom,
Dance with the shadows, and chase away gloom!

## A Melody of Freshness and Light

Silly ducks dance in a row,
Waddling fast, oh the show!
Sunshine giggles on the ground,
Ticklish grass, joy unbound.

Bicycles wobble, bells ring loud,
A cat in a hat yells, 'Look at me, proud!'
Lemonade spills, laughter flows,
Chasing clouds, see how it goes!

Butterflies in polka dots,
Play hopscotch with little tots.
A tree in bloom, its limbs all bend,
It whispers secrets, fun to lend.

With every step, a funny face,
Nature joins in the embrace.
Life's a giggle, let's not delay,
In this fresh, light-hearted array.

## Whispers of Sweetness Along the Way

Candy clouds and jelly beans,
Wobble with the playful scenes.
Lollypops on every street,
Bouncing joy, oh, what a treat!

Squirrels chatter, acorns toss,
Petty fights, oh what a loss!
In a pie, a sprinkle of fun,
Chasing echoes, everyone!

Sunshine tickles round the bend,
Where giggle-riddled voices blend.
With a wink and silly cheer,
Every sweet moment is near.

So let us stroll, without a care,
Through laughter dancing in the air.
Where every whisper holds a grin,
Join the path, let's wander in!

## Blossoms Underfoot

Step on petals, hear them pop,
Round the corner, laughter stops.
Funny hats on heads so high,
As bees buzz in a silly fly.

Puppies tumble, tails a-flap,
Caught in a flower's colorful trap.
A mischievous breeze makes branches sway,
Conspiring giggles all the way.

Frogs in bow ties croak a tune,
As daffodils dance under the moon.
Twirling leaves tickle our feet,
In this patch, pure joy we greet.

So hop along this flowery spree,
With blossoms underfoot, wild and free.
Every crunch brings a chuckle bright,
A trail of laughter, pure delight!

## **A Journey in Soft Hues**

Painted skies of purple grace,
As giggling children race.
In crayons bright, they draw their fun,
With every color, hearts are won.

A friendly turtle wears a hat,
Strolling by, oh look at that!
He makes jokes in whimsical rhymes,
Counting clouds in silly times.

Each step, a bounce, a jolly cheer,
With marshmallow fluffiness near.
In sprinkled pathways soft and sweet,
Life's a melody, a rhythmic beat.

So wander down this quirky lane,
Where laughter dances, joy's the gain.
Together we roam in hues so bright,
In a tapestry woven with pure delight.

## Nature's Embrace on the Road

Bouncing down the crooked lane,
Where flowers giggle, never plain.
A squirrel in pajamas darts,
As laughter blooms from tiny hearts.

A butterfly with polka spots,
Winks at me while I tie knots.
The trees sway like they're in a band,
While bees do the conga, oh so grand!

I trip over a playful root,
And land inside a pie, to boot.
The berries laugh, they toss and tease,
As I attempt to stop and freeze.

With every step, a new surprise,
Nature's jokes are no disguise.
I chuckle at the sun's bright face,
On this silly, joyful chase.

## A Wistful Walk through Floral Dreams

In fields where daisies wear bow ties,
I see a rabbit practicing flies.
A clover sings a cheerful tune,
As ants perform their dance at noon.

A bouncing bee, a jester bold,
Tells stories that are often told.
I chuckle as the shadows play,
In this whimsical grand ballet.

Dandelion seeds float like wishes,
While grasshoppers toss out their dishes.
A daisy cups its rosy cheeks,
As I trip over lavender peaks.

With every turn, a laugh, a cheer,
The flowers beckon, "Come right here!"
In this garden filled with grins,
Adventure starts where humor begins.

## Flourishing Fantasies and Tender Trails

Skipping down a sunny lane,
I spot a fox that sings in vain.
He claims he's found the secret code,
To make the thrift shop garden grow.

A wise old owl with glasses round,
Speaks in riddles, profound and sound.
While ladybugs do yoga moves,
In sunlit patches, they improve.

Each step I take, a flower winks,
A butterfly whispers, "Watch the jinx!"
I stumble through the jumbled weeds,
As giggling stems grant silly deeds.

Nature's here with all her tricks,
Poking fun with all her picks.
Under the sky, we laugh and play,
In this garden of a joyful ballet.

## The Joy in Ripe Discoveries

Strolling past the juicy trees,
I find a frog that laughs with ease.
He wears a crown made out of fruit,
And hops around in a fancy suit.

Clusters of berries shout and sing,
Creating chaos in pink and green.
As I taste a fig that tries to hide,
The grapes burst forth, "Come join the ride!"

The figs roll over with delightful cheer,
While apricots juggle, oh so near.
Lemons throw smiles all around,
As oranges do the twist on ground.

Each step reveals a juicy plot,
In this land where the fun is hot.
With laughter dripping from the trees,
I dance among the fruity breeze.

# Memories on the Path of Bloom

With a spring in my step, I skip a bit,
Falling on faces, I can't help but sit.
Bees buzzing loudly, a comedic dance,
I wave my arms wildly, it's my only chance.

The flowers are laughing, I hear them snort,
Telling old tales of a fruity court.
I trip on a vine, do an awkward roll,
Nature's my playground, I'm on a stroll.

A squirrel mocks me with an acorn hat,
I pretend to be royal, how about that?
Birds chirp in giggles, high up in the trees,
I swear they're all laughing, oh can't they see?

As I tumble and tumble, I hear the grass cheer,
Nature's a jester, it's perfectly clear.
Each laugh that I gather, a moment to savor,
Memories bloom, in this light-hearted favor.

## **Glimpses of a Gentle Harvest**

Walking through orchards with fruits all aglow,
I grab at a peach, but it's a pit, oh no!
The trees are all giggling, their branches a sway,
I dance like a fool, what a silly display!

Cherries chuckle, dangling like bling,
While apples smirk softly, their knowledge a fling.
I slip on a melon, what a fruity joke,
Rolling in laughter, surrounded by oak.

Lemons are pouting, too sour to care,
I tell them a joke, they lighten the air.
As each veggie winks, I give them a nod,
Harvesting joy, it's oddly facades.

With a basket of laughter, my journey's complete,
Fruits full of fun, the harvest so sweet.
In this gentle moment, under skies blue,
Life's harvest is sunny, and shares laughter too.

## Wanderlust Among the Vibrant Boughs

Beneath the great boughs, I take a wild turn,
Dodging the thorns, oh how they burn!
With a hop and a skip, I tumble once more,
The trees all giggle, "What's behind that door?"

Bananas start peeling, just for the thrill,
While oranges giggle, and ripen at will.
A wild chase ensues with plums on the run,
Each slip in the mud, oh this is such fun!

My backpack's a circus, with snacks to my right,
I trip over tomatoes, a comical sight.
Mirth drips from branches like syrupy rain,
Inside this vibrant playground, I'll dance through the pain.

Every fruit's a friend with a joke up their sleeve,
In this wanderlust dream, there's more to believe.
Surrounded by laughter, I find my true place,
Among vibrant boughs, we all share this space.

## Where Wonder and Warmth Meet

On a pathway of chuckles, in daylight so bright,
With bees doing flips, it's a funny sight.
Warmed by the sun, I giggle with glee,
Each whispering leaf calls, "Come play, it's free!"

Butterflies flutter, putting on a play,
In costumes of color, they brighten the day.
A phoenix of petals flutters so high,
With laughter, we travel, just you and I.

Jellybeans rolling, do they want to race?
Tripping on sidewalks, oh what a disgrace!
With each silly tumble, the flowers applaud,
In this place of wonder, I feel like a god.

Gathered in laughter, beneath nature's dome,
I find my heart soaring, I finally feel home.
Where warmth fills the air and joys fly in fleets,
In a world full of laughter, where wonder greets.

## Glades of Amber and Dawn

In the morning glow, I trip and slip,
Chasing shadows with a funny flip.
The frogs all giggle, they can't help but sing,
As I dance with daisies, what joys they bring.

Bees buzzing loudly, they bump and dive,
While I twirl and tumble, feeling alive.
Laughter erupts from the trees up high,
Even the clouds seem to wink and sigh.


Squirrels do somersaults, quite a sight!
As I stumble and fumble, oh what delight!
Sunbeams filter through leaves like confetti,
Life's a wild party; my dance feels so petty.

With a skip and a hop, I chase my dreams,
Frolicking through fields, bursting at the seams.
Nature's my playground; I'll take the fall,
Laughing and tumbling, I'm having a ball.

## **Glide Through Glistening Groves**

In the glistening grove, where mischief thrives,
I dodge tree branches, which dance and jive.
A chipmunk chortles, I dare to pirouette,
But gravity's tricky; I mean, what a set!

The path is slippery, gives me a fright,
As I slip on dew, oh what a sight!
Birds chuckle sweetly, they witness my plight,
Nature's a show, with pure comedic light.

Bouncing over roots like a jack-in-the-box,
I leap through the brush, avoiding the flocks.
A squirrel throws acorns, a game for us all,
Yet I twist and I tumble, too clumsy to stall.

Now I'm caught in a bind, with thorns everywhere,
Like a tangled-up ribbon, I'm caught in the air.
Yet laughter erupts as I wriggle and weave,
In this groovy maze, I dare to believe!

## **Mellow Moments on Tranquil Trails**

On mellow trails where the wildflowers bloom,
I waddle like ducks, making quite a room.
The bumblebees chuckle; they point and declare,
That I'm the goofiest traveler out here!

Sunset paints skies in shades of soft pink,
As I trip on my shoelace, and pause to rethink.
With owls hooting laughter from high up their thrones,
I stumble in rhythm, while chasing my bones.


Every step is a dance; each breath is a cheer,
But watch for low branches when they appear!
They snag on my hat, as the deer prance near,
I'm a walking slapstick—the forest's dear.

Yet nothing can stop me, I'm embracing the fun,
With giggles and chuckles as bright as the sun.
Amongst all the antics, I'm feeling so spry,
As nature's my stage, I don't think I'll cry!

## The Golden Embrace of Nature

The sun hugs the horizon, in golden embrace,
While I navigate trickles, my own little race.
In the river of laughter, I catch my foot,
Splashing and slipping—oh, what a hoot!

That mischief-filled brook sings its watery tune,
As I paddle and prance under the watchful moon.
Butterflies giggle, parade on the wing,
While I leap like a fool, oh what joy they bring!

Beneath the tall trees, I dramatically stumble,
Hoping I won't fall in that big pile of fumble.
With wildflowers cheering my every mistake,
I make nature laugh, for goodness' sake!

In this golden embrace, hilarity swells,
With humor and joy—nature casts its spells.
As I tumble and trip, a true work of art,
In this wild wonderland, I play my part.

## The Charm of Lush Byways

Wandering down the winding lane,
I tripped on roots, but felt no pain.
With every step, a fruit's surprise,
A juicy drop, right from the skies.

With giggles rolling, I took a bite,
The sweetness made my day feel bright.
A squirrel chuckled, tossed a cheer,
As sticky fingers drew me near.

The bushes danced, the flowers pranced,
A buzzing bee was quite entranced.
My hat flew off, the breeze took flight,
I chased it down—what a delight!

When friends arrived, we formed a line,
With fruity hats, we laughed divine.
In this wild patch, our hearts did sway,
Embracing dreams in playful play.

## Under the Shade of Abundance

With hats adorned, we bask and lounge,
Under trees where shadows crouch.
A picnic spread, with treats to share,
And funny stories fill the air.

A sandwich flopped, then rolled away,
A curious duck came out to play.
We laughed until we snorted loud,
As chips flew high, our hearts so proud.

Pinecones dropped like little bombs,
Engagement games of nature's charms.
With laughter leaping, we all cheered,
For every mishap that appeared.

As sunlight danced, the shadows grew,
On this day, our joy just grew.
Under leafy roofs, we sigh and grin,
With every shenanigan, new fun begins.

## Sipping Sweetness from the Air

With straws that bent, we sip delight,
On breezes thickening with the night.
Each bubble popping, made us grin,
   As flavors burst, we drank it in.

A fruit parade came waltzing by,
A lemon juggling, oh my, oh my!
The cantaloupe wore shades so cool,
A dancing pleasure, sweet, not cruel.

Remember when the pudding spilled?
Big giggles came, our laughter filled.
We scooped it up, a chocolate race,
   With smiles spread across each face.

The skies turned pink, the stars awoke,
We froze mid-laugh, the spoon a joke.
In sweetness reigned, our hearts afloat,
   As tales of fun, we gladly wrote.

## Laughter Echoes in the Grove

In the grove where chuckles bloom,
A tarzan swing—oh, what a zoom!
I soared with glee, then landed wrong,
In bushes green, where I belong.

With watermelon seeds, we planned a fight,
Heaven's missiles in summer light.
A splash of juice, then running fast,
Our giggles echoed, a spell was cast.

A raccoon peeked, with curious eyes,
We offered him a grand surprise.
Together we shared a fruity snack,
In nature's arms, there's no looking back.

As evening fell, with hearts aglow,
We painted skies with tales to show.
In laughter's grip, forever brave,
We dance in joy, the grove, our rave!

## Golden Dreams on Dusty Roads

On a path where dreams collide,
I tripped on fruit and nearly cried.
The sun was shining, quite a show,
But oh, those slippery stones below!

A wandering squirrel stole my cap,
I chased him on a whimsical map.
With laughter loud, I lost my way,
Found a pie shop where I'd stay!

Each bite of peach, a fit of glee,
I thought, maybe eat more than three?
The road was dusty, the fun was sweet,
Who knew a stumble could taste so neat?

So here's to dreams on rocky trails,
Where every laugh and fruit never fails.
Just watch your step, or you might see,
That life's a peach, just like me!

## The Orchard's Whisper

In a grove where giggles grow,
I heard the trees whispering low.
They told me jokes wrapped in sweet air,
About a cat who danced with flair!

A squirrel in shades, with style so grand,
Had a dance-off, wasn't he planned?
With every twist, a fruit did fall,
We laughed and slipped, oh my, what a sprawl!

The apples chuckled, plums did grin,
As nuts did roll, and chaos begin.
There's joy in fruit, a wacky charm,
Where nature's pranks do no real harm.

So if you wander through leaves so green,
Prepare for laughter like you've never seen!
The orchard's secrets, fun and bright,
Will turn your day into pure delight!

## Serenity in Stone Fruits

Among the stones where laughter blooms,
A peach once sparked a dance in rooms.
I stepped right in, my foot a mess,
Now I'm the king of fruitfulness!

A berry brigade pranced all around,
With giggles that echoed, sweet and sound.
Peaches joined with a juicy cheer,
While cherries threw a party near!

With every slip and stumble wide,
A symphony of grins and pride.
For in this fruit-filled crazy spree,
Life's juiciest laughs are wild and free!

So grab a bowl and have a feast,
Where every pit is humor's beast.
You never know what joys await,
In the calm of stones that create fate!

## Sweet Steps Beneath the Blossoms

Beneath the blooms, I dared to roam,
With petals falling, it felt like home.
But oh, the bees had plans of their own,
As I tripped on roots, they'd drone and moan!

A waltz with bees, I jested with flair,
While dodging fruits tossed in the air.
I juggled apples, it was a sight,
Till one rolled off, I took flight!

The blossoms giggled—oh, what a scene,
As I swirled 'round, a peachy machine.
With colors bright and spirits high,
I danced through petals, and time did fly!

So if you wander 'neath fragrant skies,
Take a moment to laugh, and just be wise.
For in the blossoms, fun's not shy,
And sweet mischief will surely comply!

## Orchard-Woven Journeys

In a grove where fruit hangs low,
Squirrels plot their daring show.
One steals a peach, oh what a stunt,
While others munch, they laugh and grunt.

Beneath the trees, a picnic lies,
Ants march in with eager eyes.
They spiral up a blanket's fold,
To claim the jam; so brave, so bold.

A bee buzzed past, in quite a mood,
Dancing near the sweetened food.
He stole a sip, and then a jig,
That little bee was quite the big.

So gather round, embrace the fun,
In orchards bright, we've only begun.
With every bite, a laugh will sprout,
Our joyful journey's what it's about.

## Sunkissed Escapades

Beneath a sunbeam's playful glance,
We chase each other in a dance.
Slipping on juice, we slide and spin,
Let the fruity games begin!

Wobbly legs and sticky hands,
As laughter sparkles, life expands.
"Catch that peach!" someone will shout,
In a tug-of-war, it's what we're about.

A rogue critter claims a prize,
It zooms away; oh, the surprise!
We follow close, but then we trip,
In this orchard, we flip and dip.

So grab your friends, don't be polite,
Join the games from day to night.
With sunshine bright and fruit to share,
Our silly escapades fill the air.

## Serenity in Ripened Boughs

Under branches, shadows play,
In this refuge, we'll stay all day.
A hammock swings, full of delight,
With giggles echoing, oh what a sight.

Sipping juice, we share our dreams,
While squirrels laugh at silly schemes.
A tug on the rope sends us both,
Sailing high, oh what a growth!

The breeze whispers funny tales,
Of fruit-filled boats with no more sails.
As laughter spills from every mouth,
We're sailing south, or maybe north?

In this haven, peace ignites,
With fruity fun, our hearts take flight.
So let us bask in juicy cheer,
Our cozy life, forever dear.

## Paths Adorned with Blush

The trail before us, oh so bright,
Adorned with blush, a lovely sight.
We prance and hop, like silly ducks,
Dreaming up plans while laughter clucks.

A friendly wager leads the way,
Who can stack the most, they say?
With juicy fruit in armfuls, we go,
Balancing high, putting on a show.

But oh! A tumble, a juicy splash,
As fruit cascades in wild, bold crash.
We roll and giggle, what a scene,
With sticky faces, we grab the greens.

So let us stroll these merry trails,
Where every stumble surely prevails.
With friends beside, our joys combine,
In these blush-clad paths, we shine!

## **Blossoms in the Breeze**

In a garden where giggles play,
Butterflies flirt, oh what a day!
Petals dance like they know a secret,
Swaying to jokes that they all beget.

Sunshine tickles the grass just right,
Ants in top hats strutting with delight.
Bees buzz tunes that make flowers chuckle,
As bunnies hop, their ears in a shuffle.

Caterpillars green with envy sigh,
Watching the ladybugs flutter by.
Their polka-dot parties so full of cheer,
Who knew gardening could be this queer?

On this path where the laughter blooms,
Nature's a stage where joy resumes.
A stroll through petals, a giggle or two,
In this whimsical realm, there's fun anew!

## Sunlit Trails of Ambrosia

Sunbeams sprinkle like sugar on leaves,
Laughter erupts where the wildflower weaves.
Sassy squirrels throw acorns like darts,
While turtles in shades are the coolest of arts.

Lemonade rivers flow down grassy hills,
Where frogs in tuxedos take comedy spills.
A chicken on a skateboard zooms with a shout,
As the daisies all cheer, "Show us what you're about!"

Sunrise paints faces in colors so bright,
A parade of quirks, what a marvelous sight!
The path is a giggle, the sky's a grand stage,
No dull moments here, just a joy-filled page.

From fruit-filled trees to laughter's sweet chase,
Every step in this place is a smile on your face.
Dance with the daisies, swing with the breeze,
In these dazzling trails, life's laughter's the keys!

**Nectar on the Wind**

Whispers of sweetness drift through the air,
Honeybees gossip without a care.
With jokes in their stingers and puns on their wings,
They buzz around as the whole garden sings.

A lizard in shades sunbathes with flair,
While ants in a conga line jig without a care.
The daisies complain it's too loud for their tastes,
But the dandelions dance, filling up with grace.

Winds of hilarity tickle the grass,
As clouds in the sky play a comedic class.
One drifts too low, gets caught in a tree,
As it shakes with laughter, "Oh, what can it be?"

With every gust comes a new pun to share,
Life's a quirky adventure, filled with flair.
Nature's comic club is always in session,
Join in the laughter, it's a sweet obsession!

## Juicy Journeys of the Heart

In the orchard of giggles, where dreams take flight,
Cherries in helmets race into the night.
Their juicy stories spill over with glee,
As plump peaches roll, "Come play with me!"

A road paved with jellybeans leads the way,
Where laughter-studded cobbles invite you to stay.
Here, fruit flies joke with the ripe, bursting pears,
Trading their secrets like old millionaires.

The moon jumps up, sporting a silly grin,
As figs wear sunglasses, "Let the fun begin!"
Today's agenda involves a wacky parade,
With oranges tossing confetti, unafraid.

In this realm where sweetness knows no end,
Every corner turned finds a fruit-loving friend.
So hop on this journey, let joy depart,
It's a festival of laughter straight from the heart!

www.ingramcontent.com/pod-product-compliance
Lightning Source LLC
Chambersburg PA
CBHW071127130526
44590CB00056B/2815